Bible reflections
for older people

BRF

The Bible Reading Fellowship
15 The Chambers, Vineyard
Abingdon OX14 3FE
brf.org.uk

The Bible Reading Fellowship (BRF) is a Registered Charity (233280)

ISBN 978 0 85746 514 6
First published 2016
10 9 8 7 6 5 4 3 2 1 0
All rights reserved

Acknowledgements
Scripture quotations marked NIV are taken from The Holy Bible, New International Version (Anglicised edition), copyright © 1979, 1984, 2011 by Biblica. Used by permission of Hodder & Stoughton Publishers, an Hachette UK company. All rights reserved. 'NIV' is a registered trademark of Biblica. UK trademark number 1448790.

Scripture quotations marked CEV are taken from the Contemporary English Version. New Testament © American Bible Society 1991, 1992, 1995. Old Testament © American Bible Society 1995. Anglicisations © British & Foreign Bible Society 1996. Used by permission.

Scripture quotations marked NLT are taken from the Holy Bible, New Living Translation, copyright © 1996, 2004, 2007, 2013. Used by permission of Tyndale House Publishers, Inc., Carol Stream, Illinois 60188. All rights reserved.

Scripture quotations marked NRSV are taken from the New Revised Standard Version of the Bible, Anglicised edition, copyright © 1989, 1995 by the Division of Christian Education of the National Council of the Churches of Christ in the United States of America. Used by permission. All rights reserved.

Scripture quotations marked KJV are taken from the Authorised Version of the Bible (The King James Bible), the rights in which are vested in the Crown, and are reproduced by permission of the Crown's Patentee, Cambridge University Press.

Scripture quotations marked MSG are taken from *THE MESSAGE*. Copyright © 1993, 1994, 1995, 1996, 2000, 2001, 2002. Used by permission of NavPress Publishing Group.

Cover and images on pp.31 and 35 © Thinkstock

Every effort has been made to trace and contact copyright owners for material used in this resource. We apologise for any inadvertent omissions or errors, and would ask those concerned to contact us so that full acknowledgement can be made in the future.

A catalogue record for this book is available from the British Library

Printed by Gutenberg Press, Tarxien, Malta

Contents

About the writers

 David Winter is a former producer and Head of Religious Broadcasting at the BBC. He is also the author of 43 books, the most recent being *Heaven's Morning: Rethinking the destination* (BRF, 2016). Now retired from full-time ministry, he lives in Berkshire.

 Jennifer Bute is a former medical missionary and a retired GP. She is now living with dementia and is a champion for others who are facing this challenge. She speaks at conferences and on radio, and has been involved in television programmes raising awareness and understanding of this illness. Her website **www.gloriousopportunity.org** brings encouragement and support to thousands.

 Lin Ball's career began in journalism over 40 years ago. Highlights include interviewing missionaries for OMF, editing Bible resources with Scripture Union for over twelve years, creating radio programmes about disability, and helping a friend write and publish his story weeks before cancer claimed his earthly life.

 Russ Parker was Director of the Acorn Christian Healing Foundation for 18 years before founding 2Restore, a resource for reconciliation and renewal for wounded churches. He is an author and travels extensively as a conference speaker. He is married to Roz and has two children, Emma and Joel. He supports Liverpool Football Club and lives in Surrey.

From the Editor

Welcome! We hope you will find the Bible reflections in the following pages helpful and encouraging.

In this first issue **David Winter** writes about the challenge of change. In his series **Changing times,** he reminds us that God knows our future and we are safe in his care. **Jennifer Bute**, herself facing the challenges of living with dementia, helps us celebrate the **Joy for the journey** that God offers us all. This time of life often brings the need for decisions and help with guidance. **Lin Ball** in her series **Decisions, decisions...** points us back to the One who knows the answers, encouraging us to take our concerns to God. And **Russ Parker**, in his series **Rhythms of remembrance**, speaks to us of memories and remembrance—and the joy and blessing these can bring, as we turn to the One who chooses to remember you and me.

In the centre pages, **Debbie Thrower** of **BRF's The Gift of Years** ministry brings stories, ideas and encouragement. We hope you will enjoy reading these and hearing from others who may be facing similar issues to your own.

We'd love to hear from you about how these reflections may be helping you. Please get in touch using the contact details supplied on the order forms at the end of this resource.
Meanwhile, our prayer is that, as you spend time with God, you will know his presence and discover more about the Lord Jesus, who doesn't change, but is 'the same yesterday and today and for ever' (Hebrews 13:8, NIV).

God bless you,

Tricia Williams

Using these reflections

Perhaps you have always had a special daily time for reading the Bible and praying. But now, as you grow older, you are finding it more difficult to keep to a regular pattern or find it hard to concentrate. Or maybe you've never done this before. Whatever your situation, these Bible reflections aim to help you take a few moments to read God's word and pray, whenever you are able.

When to read them

You can read these Bible reflections in the morning or last thing at night, or any time during the day. Why not use them as a way of making 'an appointment to chat with God'?

There are 40 daily Bible reflections, grouped around four themes. Each one includes some verses from the Bible, a reflection to help you in your own thinking about God and a suggestion for prayer. The reflections aren't dated, so it doesn't matter if you're not able to read them every day. The Bible verses are printed, but if you'd like to read from your own Bible, that's fine too.

How to read them

- **Take time** to quieten yourself, becoming aware of God's presence, asking him to speak to you through the Bible and the reflection.

- **Read** the Bible verses and the reflection:

  - What do you especially like or find helpful in these verses?

  - What might God be saying to you through this reading?

  - Is there something to pray about or thank God for?

- **Pray**. Each reflection includes a prayer suggestion. You might like to pray for yourself or take the opportunity to think about and pray for others.

Changing times

David Winter

'Change and decay in all around I see,' says the hymn-writer.* Well, I'm not sure about the decay, but change is everywhere! Anyone over 50 has lived through an era of huge changes in the way we live. It's hard to credit, but 40 years ago there were no cash machines, computers, mobile phones, internet, world wide web or email. Cataract and bypass operations were rare and difficult. There were no women vicars, let alone bishops!

On the whole, people have taken to most of those changes quite happily. The changes we find more difficult—and which are also more frequent in modern life—are those that affect our private or domestic lives: moving home because we need to be near our children, who may live far away, even in another country; living with a medical condition or limited mobility, so that we can't drive a car or go out on our own. And, perhaps most powerfully, the death of cherished friends and relatives, whose companionship and love cannot easily be replaced.

To live is, in fact, to cope with change, from childhood to old age. It doesn't make it easier, but at least it's a shared experience. And it's one about which the Bible has some wise and wonderful things to say, as we shall see.

* Henry Francis Lyte, 1793–1847, 'Abide with Me'

Genesis 12:1–4 (NRSV)

On the move

Now the Lord said to Abram, 'Go from your country and your kindred and your father's house to the land that I will show you. I will make of you a great nation, and I will bless you, and make your name great, so that you will be a blessing… and in you all the families of the earth shall be blessed.' So Abram went, as the Lord had told him; and Lot went with him. Abram was seventy-five years old when he departed from Haran.

Many of the older people at my church have, like me, moved here to be near sons or daughters. Often it's a big step to take. Some have left a lifelong home to make a new start in an unfamiliar area: new friends, new environment, new doctor and so on. The positive side is that they have moved to be with their 'kindred', unlike Abram, who was called to leave his familiar country, his kindred and his 'father's house' to start an entirely new life. He was obeying a prompting from God to go to an unknown destination. That's to say, it was unknown to Abram, but clearly God knew where he wanted Abram to be, and why.

Abram's obedience to this divine prompting would have immeasurable consequences. He would be the 'father' of a great nation. He would be blessed and honoured. And in him 'all the families of the earth' would be blessed. Obediently he left the family home in Haran and, accompanied by his wife Sarai and his nephew Lot, made his way to the place God had chosen for him.

■ PRAYER

God of the present and the future, remind me that what is unknown to me is known to you. Amen

Psalm 77:4–8a (NRSV)

A steadfast God...

You keep my eyelids from closing; I am so troubled that I cannot speak. I consider the days of old, and remember the years of long ago. I commune with my heart in the night; I meditate and search my spirit: 'Will the Lord spurn for ever, and never again be favourable? Has his steadfast love ceased for ever?'

This psalm is the desperate prayer of an older person. They lie in bed at night, regretting 'the years of long ago', the 'days of old', when they experienced God's blessing. What has happened? Why are things now like this? No wonder the writer 'communes with his heart in the night', and finds it hard to sleep. One wonders what particular events or changes in his life have caused this spiritual setback.

The clue may be in the reference to 'days of old'. It's a familiar experience for those of us who are older. We speak a lot, perhaps too much, about 'then'—the 'good old days'—and the unfamiliar newness of 'now'. I sometimes think we should ban the word 'nowadays' from our conversations once we are past, say, 60, because it's invariably followed by something we don't approve of: noisy children, litter in the streets, disrespect for cherished traditions.

But 'nowadays' is where we are. We are called to love and serve God *now*, however much the scenery has changed. Later in this psalm (see vv. 11–15) the writer recognises that the God who has blessed in times past is the same God who is with us now. 'Steadfast love' means what it says.

■ **PRAYER**

Heavenly Father, your love for me is 'steadfast'. Help me to trust you in times of change and anxiety. Amen

Hebrews 13:5–6, 8, 13–14 (NRSV)

Yesterday, today, for ever...

Keep your lives free from the love of money, and be content with what you have; for he has said, 'I will never leave you or forsake you.' So we can say with confidence, 'The Lord is my helper; I will not be afraid. What can anyone do to me?'... Jesus Christ is the same yesterday and today and for ever... Let us then go to him outside the camp and bear the abuse he endured. For here we have no lasting city, but we are looking for the city that is to come.

The Bible tells a single story, of a God of 'steadfast love' who has in his Son Jesus shown his people the wonderful extent of that love. God has not abandoned them. Far from 'leaving' or 'forsaking' them, he has come among his people in his beloved Son.

What is true of their God is also true of their Saviour, Jesus Christ. He is the same, 'yesterday and today and for ever'. And what was true for those early Jewish Christians is equally true for us today. This is the Christian confidence—not in ourselves, but in God and his Son Jesus, who do not change with the passing of earthly time. As the old children's chorus says, 'All may change, but Jesus never!'

Jesus was abused and died outside the city walls of Jerusalem (the writer compares it to the tabernacle in the wilderness, 'the camp'). We take our stand with him, recognising that our lasting home is not on earth, but in the heavenly city, the new Jerusalem (Revelation 21:2).

■ **PRAYER**
Unchanging Lord, be with me in all the changes and chances of this mortal life. Amen

Ephesians 4:14–16 (NRSV)

True maturity

We must no longer be children, tossed to and fro and blown about by every wind of doctrine, by people's trickery, by their craftiness in deceitful scheming. But speaking the truth in love, we must grow up in every way into him who is the head, into Christ, from whom the whole body, joined and knitted together by every ligament with which it is equipped, as each part is working properly, promotes the body's growth in building itself up in love.

I don't suppose the Christians at Ephesus appreciated being called 'children'! Of course, the apostle isn't talking about calendar age, but maturity of character. They were too easily swayed and 'blown about' by the 'latest thing', too susceptible to people who simply wanted to lead them astray.

What he wanted them to do was 'grow up'! However old they were in years, they should embrace a more mature approach to their faith. After all, they were not simply individuals making up their minds about different possibilities. They belonged to Christ. They had been baptised into his body, the Church. There they could find the maturity he desired for them.

Modern society is a bit like a religious supermarket, with everyone peddling their wares. It can be deeply unsettling, even for lifelong Christians. The apostle Paul's answer is, quite simply, the Church. We learn from each other, we grow together, we support and help each other. As the saying goes, 'Better together!'

■ PRAYER
Lord, in the fellowship of the Church, may I be one who helps others, and in turn am willing to be helped. Amen

Ecclesiastes 3:1–4, 11 (NRSV)

For everything a season...

For everything there is a season… a time to be born, and a time to die; a time to plant, and a time to pluck up what is planted; a time to kill, and a time to heal; a time to break down, and a time to build up; a time to weep, and a time to laugh; a time to mourn, and a time to dance… [God] has made everything suitable for its time; moreover, he has put a sense of past and future into their minds, yet they cannot find out what God has done from the beginning to the end.

Perhaps you recognise these words from Pete Seeger's 1960s song 'Turn, Turn, Turn', later a number one hit for the folk rock band The Byrds. Its popularity possibly arose from its association with the traumatic events of the time, including the Vietnam War and the nuclear threat. Today, there are different anxieties.

The message of Ecclesiastes is a call to godly wisdom, to get our priorities right, to see that 'God has made everything suitable for its time'. The modern world rebels against the idea of the passing of time. It resents getting old, and the idea of mortality. Yet a 'sense of past and future' is a vital ingredient of life as God has created it.

As we get older and look back on our lives, we recognise the wisdom in these words. We have all known times of weeping and days of laughter; periods of mourning and times of celebration. Faith in God, the one who created time and seasons, makes sense of what otherwise can seem like random events.

■ **PRAYER**

Lord, help me to see that, one day, times and seasons will end, caught up in your eternal life and love. Amen

Luke 1:35–38 (NRSV)

Facing life's surprises

The angel said to her, 'The Holy Spirit will come upon you, and the power of the Most High will overshadow you; therefore the child to be born will be holy; he will be called Son of God. And now, your relative Elizabeth in her old age has also conceived a son; and this is the sixth month for her who was said to be barren. For nothing will be impossible with God.' Then Mary said, 'Here am I, the servant of the Lord; let it be with me according to your word.'

The familiarity of this story, read every Christmas, may mean that we miss its true impact. It records experiences of profound shock for two women. One, of course, was Mary, a young woman betrothed to the village carpenter in Nazareth; the other was Elizabeth, the much older wife of a temple priest, Zechariah. Both were not expecting pregnancy, Mary because she was still a virgin, and Elizabeth because, having passed childbearing age, she was assumed to be 'barren'. However, as the angel says, 'Nothing will be impossible with God,' and what seemed impossible happened. Elizabeth, in her 'old age', was already six months pregnant. And Mary became pregnant, just as the angel had promised. But who would believe her story? It took a divine dream to persuade her fiancé to proceed with their marriage.

What Luke wants us to recognise is not the problems these promises brought with them, but the simple, trusting response of both women. Mary, the Lord's 'servant', simply accepted God's will, and so did the faithful older woman.

■ PRAYER

Lord, surprises and shocks do come in life. Help me, with Mary, simply to pray, 'Your will be done.' Amen

2 Timothy 4:9–16 (NRSV)

Where are my friends?

Do your best to come to me soon, for Demas, in love with this present world, has deserted me and gone to Thessalonica; Crescens has gone to Galatia, Titus to Dalmatia. Only Luke is with me. Get Mark and bring him with you, for he is useful in my ministry. I have sent Tychicus to Ephesus. When you come, bring the cloak that I left with Carpus at Troas, also the books, and above all the parchments. Alexander the coppersmith did me great harm… At my first defence no one came to my support, but all deserted me.

Sooner or later, most of us experience what the apostle Paul is feeling here. Where is everyone when I need them? All those friends of yesteryear, the people I relied on, the ones who cheered me up when I was down? I must say I love this strangely vulnerable plea, tacked on to the end of a rather formal letter. It's a rare glimpse into Paul the older man, facing the possibility of imminent death and suddenly feeling lonely. Mind you, I can hardly forgive him for 'Only Luke is with me'—*only?*—his loyal and long-term friend, and a *doctor*!

Still, we can guess from this that no one, not even the great apostle, is exempt from a bit of self-pity and loneliness—he's feeling the winter chill, too, and missing his books! It's not the *feeling* that's the problem, but what we do about it. Paul goes on to say, 'But the Lord stood by me and gave me strength' (v. 17). He may have *felt* alone, but in the deepest possible way he knew he wasn't.

■ PRAYER

Lord Jesus, you promised to be with us to the end of time. Help me to trust your promise. Amen

Proverbs 3:1–3, 5–6 (NRSV)

Trust in the LORD

My child, do not forget my teaching, but let your heart keep my commandments; for length of days and years of life and abundant welfare they will give you. Do not let loyalty and faithfulness forsake you; bind them round your neck, write them on the tablet of your heart... Trust in the LORD with all your heart, and do not rely on your own insight. In all your ways acknowledge him, and he will make straight your paths.

With its promise of abundant welfare and 'straight paths', the key to these great verses is the word 'LORD'. When the holy name is printed in capital letters in the Bible it translates the most holy name of God. In fact, it's so holy that it could not be spelt out. It speaks of the eternal, changeless God, the I AM who simply exists, without beginning or end. 'Holy and awesome is his name' (Psalm 111:9, NRSV).

To trust in such a God is to accept that he knows best. What is the point of being 'wise in our own eyes' when through trusting and honouring God we can be guided by him? Here we are offered a straight choice, a clear question of priority. Are we going to keep stumbling on, thinking we know best, trusting our own 'insights', or are we going to 'trust in the LORD with all our hearts' and allow him to 'make straight our paths'? It's not an easy surrender, and we shall probably from time to time stray from it, but God will honour our intention to remember his teaching and keep his commandments. And just look at the rewards!

■ **PRAYER**

Help me, Lord, in 'all my ways' to acknowledge you and so let you direct my path. Amen

Psalm 62:1–2, 7 (NRSV)

Clinging to the rock

For God alone my soul waits in silence; from him comes my salvation. He alone is my rock and my salvation, my fortress; I shall never be shaken… On God rests my deliverance and my honour; my mighty rock, my refuge is in God.

If you read these verses in the light of the whole psalm you will see that they are a defiant assertion of faith in God when things are bad. Many of us will have found this—when the clouds gathered we began to discover the light of God; when everything seemed to be against us we learnt that God is on our side. The psalmist repeats the word 'alone'. In his desperate need, there was simply nowhere else to turn.

Yet, in that time of need, God proved to be everything he needed. God is his 'rock', and you can't shift rocks easily! God is his 'refuge', a hiding place from the storm. God is a fortress, where the arrows of his enemies can't penetrate. Twice we are told that God is his 'salvation', by which he means that God rescues and restores him. It's quite a catalogue of blessings!

A surprising thing, maybe, is that they come to him as he 'waits in silence'. It's easy to assume that there was little silence in the worship of the temple—more percussion than peace! But clearly the psalmist knew the precious secret of silence. I confess that I find achieving it elusive. Stray thoughts and ideas distract me. Yet I also know that God's invitation is clear: 'Be *still*, and know that I am God' (Psalm 46:10, NRSV).

■ **PRAYER**

When things get tough, Lord, help me to cling to 'my mighty rock'. Amen

Psalm 121:1–2, 5–8 (NRSV)

Going out and coming in

I lift up my eyes to the hills—from where will my help come? My help comes from the LORD, who made heaven and earth… The LORD is your keeper; the LORD is your shade at your right hand. The sun shall not strike you by day, nor the moon by night. The LORD will keep you from all evil; he will keep your life. The LORD will keep your going out and your coming in from this time on and for evermore.

Once again, the drumbeat of these verses is a constant calling out to 'the LORD' (capital letters!). It's not to the 'hills' we should look for help, like the pagans, but to the Eternal One who made sky and earth. He is our 'help' when we need it and our 'keeper' when we get lost. He is our parasol, shielding us from the heat of the midday sun. He also offers shade from the moon—the ancient world was very scared of being 'moonstruck'. In fact, the LORD will keep his people from 'all evil'. To 'keep your life' means to make your days good and fulfilling.

Then there is the final promise. The LORD will keep your 'going out and coming in'. This is one of the 'psalms of ascent', which were sung by pilgrims as they made their way up to Jerusalem (and it was definitely 'up'). They had left their homes far away, 'gone out' to make their pilgrimage to the Holy City. Eventually they would 'come in' to the great temple, to the worship, the prayers and the singing. Going out or coming in, the LORD would be with them.

■ **PRAYER**

As I make my own pilgrim journey to the Holy City, please watch over my goings out and in. Amen

Joy for the journey

Jennifer Bute

As we get older we may become less mobile or independent—and it's easy to think things were much better when we were younger and to feel sad about what we have lost. We may have failing memory, feel neglected, not be sure about our place in society, or be struggling with ill health. Jesus knew about loss of independence and pain in his last days too, being and feeling deserted. Yet he was still aware of others, caring for them, while continuing to fulfil his purpose—to bring about our reconciliation with God.

The spiritual never dies. God loves and accepts us no matter what the state of our minds, brains or bodies. The psalmist David writes:

> *Restore to me the joy of your salvation*
> *and grant me a willing spirit, to sustain me.*
> **Psalm 51:12, NIV**

It *is* possible still to know joy in the midst of tough times—but we also need a willing spirit to keep us steady through those tough times. Over the last year I've been encouraged by some of the Bible passages that follow. I pray that they will encourage you too day by day.

Psalm 71:16–18 (NIV)

This is my story...

I will come and proclaim your mighty acts, Sovereign Lord; I will proclaim your righteous deeds, yours alone. Since my youth, God, you have taught me, and to this day I declare your marvellous deeds. Even when I am old and grey, do not forsake me, my God, till I declare your power to the next generation, your mighty acts to all who are to come.

We all love telling stories, whether about ourselves or other people. It amuses me that the writer of these words added 'yours alone' when talking about 'proclaiming deeds'. It is all too easy to talk about anything *except* what God has done for us! I have been amazed how people with little time for God are willing to listen to personal stories about what God has done for me.

During our lifetimes some of us may have been deserted—or certainly felt we were—and now we may wonder if God might desert us. The psalmist begs God not to forsake him when he is old. Yet he thinks it is *more* important to tell the younger generation of God's power than to be concerned about his own comfort. When we're old, we still have a responsibility to proclaim God's greatness to younger generations. Even with failing memories, we still know that God has been faithful to us. We can all tell good stories about the past—so why not tell stories about God's goodness!

■ **PRAYER**

Lord Jesus, forgive us for so often preferring to talk about what we have done rather than what you have done. Give us the courage to talk about you. Help us to inspire those who are much younger than we are to be amazed too. Amen

Psalm 119:73–77 (NIV)

Held in your hands

Your hands made me and formed me; give me understanding to learn your commands… I know, Lord, that your laws are righteous, and that in faithfulness you have afflicted me. May your unfailing love be my comfort, according to your promise to your servant. Let your compassion come to me that I may live, for your law is my delight.

Hands… Touch is so important—it can heal, convey care and love. Perhaps you have felt hands of hate and rejection too.

As a child, I loved that picture of the 'Praying Hands' painted by Albrecht Dürer, speaking of the power of prayer. Sometimes we may mourn that we were *not* always touched by kindness, or feel sad about times when there were no hands to hold. Perhaps we never knew the touch of human love. So this reminder that God's hands formed us and made us what we are is such an encouragement. His hands convey greater care and concern, and more love, than could those of any human.

Loving parents have rules and discipline their children. God does the same for us, out of love—yet even as adults we can sulk when we don't get our own way! In these verses, the psalmist wants to know God's love, his compassion and his comfort. And—whether we experience tough times caused by our own obstinacy, or because of circumstances beyond our control—*we* are held in God's loving hands. The psalmist discovers this as he finds 'delight' in God's word.

■ **PRAYER**

Jesus, you experienced the touch of cruel hands, and of those in need or despair. May we feel your touch today, whatever our present circumstances. May we even find joy in them, because you pour your love into our lives through them. Amen

Isaiah 55:1–2 (NIV)

God's welcome

'Come, all you who are thirsty, come to the waters; and you who have no money, come, buy and eat! Come, buy wine and milk without money and without cost. Why spend money on what is not bread, and your labour on what does not satisfy? Listen, listen to me, and eat what is good, and you will delight in the richest of fare.'

'Come...'—God's words of welcome contrast perhaps with painful childhood memories of the 'Go away!' or 'Don't bother me!' kind. Maybe you're even reminded of hurtful relationships later in your life when you've felt you were not wanted any more. Here is God *wanting* us to come to him.

We are startled by the command to those who have no money: 'Come, buy.' It seems a bit unkind! We so quickly jump to conclusions and assume God is unreasonable—but read on! God is calling us to a different kind of life in which money does not and cannot 'buy'. Some 'things' cost us time and emotion; and in some situations this is of greater cost than money. But God is not asking us to make any sacrifices... He has done all that on our behalf.

We have a choice. We can spend our time and efforts on what does not provide lasting worth and does not satisfy. God offers us something that does. But that involves listening to him, *coming* to him, rather than turning our backs on him and saying, 'I haven't got...'

■ **PRAYER**

Lord Jesus, we are overwhelmed by your welcome, your wanting *us to come to you, your insistence on the things of lasting value. Help us to let go of the things that will not last and have open hands for the riches you want to pour on us. Amen*

Psalm 63:5–7 (NIV)

Sleepless nights

I will be satisfied as with the richest of foods; with singing lips my mouth will praise you. On my bed I remember you; I think of you through the watches of the night. Because you are my help, I sing in the shadow of your wings.

This psalm really encourages me! It begins as if all is well. Then it goes on to talk about remembering God 'through the watches of the night'… when I am in bed… when I am not able to sleep… when I am having a disturbed night! Many of us have those! Yet the psalmist is still thankful. He seems to understand his sleeplessness as an opportunity to remember God—and he still has the ability to sing in the shadows. Personally, I try to listen to music or hymns to soothe me, and use my 'energy' to pray for other people, rather than worry about not sleeping.

I know for myself that, when things are bleak, I sing, because that seems to refocus life and enable me to get back on track. Recently when things 'fell apart', I listened to a recording of the song 'Give thanks with a grateful heart'* and was reminded that it is not *just* about giving thanks. We also need a *grateful heart*—not for circumstances, but because of God's love for us. No matter what our situation, it is this that enables us to 'sing in the shadow'.

■ PRAYER

Father God, we thank you for all the help you are to us and for opportunities where we can experience your resources. When life is tough, may we know your help and be able to sing and experience joy. Please help us to be able to do that today. Amen

* Don Moen, 1986

Isaiah 55:12–13 (NIV)

Joy for tomorrow

You will go out in joy and be led forth in peace; the mountains and hills will burst into song before you, and all the trees of the field will clap their hands. Instead of the thorn-bush will grow the juniper, and instead of briers the myrtle will grow. This will be for the Lord's renown, for an everlasting sign, that will endure for ever.

As I get older, I sometimes see scripture differently. I wondered if these verses could also refer to our leaving this world, to help us face the end days or years of our lives with joy and peace.

Perhaps no one has ever rejoiced over you, or clapped their hands with enthusiasm as you go by! Here the writer claims that the time will come when things and places that we take for granted will burst into song. Heaven will be so different! I am reminded of Jesus saying that if his disciples had not praised him, the stones would have cried out (Luke 19:40).

Instead of the thorns of our existence here—whether due to health, family or circumstance—there *will* be joy and peace and good things that last for ever. And that's not just so we can feel comfortable, but for the Lord's 'renown', his amazing reputation.

■ **PRAYER**
Father God, we thank you that we have so much to look forward to. When life is tough and joy is scarce, may we remember that you are still leading us through these times. When we feel scratched, irritated and wounded by life, help us to remember that in heaven there will be no pain or sorrow. Amen

Numbers 11:1–6, 18–20 (NIV)

The good old days

Now the people complained about their hardships in the hearing of the Lord… Then fire from the Lord… consumed some of the outskirts of the camp… and again the Israelites started wailing… 'If only we had meat to eat! We remember the fish we ate in Egypt… the cucumbers, melons, leeks, onions and garlic… we never see anything but this manna!'… Now the Lord will give you meat… until… you loathe it—because you have rejected the Lord, who is among you…

The Israelites were on a difficult desert journey as they escaped from Egypt, surviving on a diet of 'manna' (v. 6). Now, where there should have been praise and worship for God's provision, complaining takes over. God was furious and sent fire, which 'consumed… the outskirts of the camp'. It doesn't say that anyone was hurt, but implies material damage. Yet the people did not learn. Again they complained that their food was boring, repetitive and without the variety they had enjoyed in Egypt. God heard and gave them what they wanted, and, as a result, many died (vv. 33–34).

We can look back with rose-tinted spectacles, complaining that life was more 'fun' in the good old days, particularly when we weren't hindered by reduced mobility or other reduced abilities. The children of Israel had forgotten to be grateful for God's love and care through the daily provision of manna. Maybe there's a reminder here for us to be grateful for the daily faithfulness of our loving heavenly Father.

■ PRAYER

Father, forgive us when we complain that our life is not as good as in the past and we are wearied by the mundane repetition of each day. Thank you for your constant love and for inner daily resources that are new every morning. Amen

Jeremiah 38:6–7, 11–13 (NIV)

Grateful for old rags

They lowered Jeremiah by ropes into the cistern; it had no water in it, only mud, and Jeremiah sank down into the mud. But Ebed-Melek… took some old rags and worn-out clothes… and let them down with ropes to Jeremiah in the cistern… 'Put these… under your arms to pad the ropes.' Jeremiah did so, and they pulled him up with the ropes and lifted him out of the cistern.

Jeremiah, the Old Testament prophet, had been thrown into a dark, damp, disgusting cistern where he 'sank down into the mud'. He had not done anything wrong. In fact, he had been put there for obeying God… telling people the truth, which they did not like. His life was in danger (v. 9). When he was rescued he would certainly have been very grateful for the provision of rags to lessen the pain as he was hauled up. These were all his rescuer could find.

We can also find ourselves in difficult situations through no fault of our own, even for doing the right thing. These can be dark places with little prospect of escape. Others may offer us the best they can. It might not be much and we have to choose whether to accept or to be grateful. Sometimes, perhaps, we don't share or give to others because we are ashamed of how little we have to offer. Jeremiah did not object to the rags—they saved his life. We need to be willing to give what we do have, even in times of our own hardship.

■ PRAYER

Lord Jesus, help me to be grateful for the rags that others might give me; make me willing to offer others what little I might have at this time. Amen

Psalm 30:8–12 (NIV)

Dancing for joy

To the Lord I cried for mercy: 'What is gained if I am silenced, if I go down to the pit? Will the dust praise you? Will it proclaim your faithfulness? Hear, Lord, and be merciful to me; Lord, be my help.' You turned my wailing into dancing; you removed my sackcloth and clothed me with joy, that my heart may sing your praises and not be silent. Lord my God, I will praise you for ever.

It's difficult to wail (or mourn) while you are dancing! Dancing takes energy, so when we are emotionally exhausted or feeling sad, it's hard to dance for joy. Here's good news—these verses teach us that when we turn to God and ask for his help, he removes our 'sackcloth' and clothes us with joy. We are not left exposed by what's gone on before or by what caused our sorrow.

It certainly is true that if we are happy, the difficult things that go on around us are less likely to affect us. But God's help is not just about making us feel good with 'warm fuzzy feelings'! The joy that he gives should overflow in praise. Have you experienced that—being so full of joy or thankfulness to God that you cannot remain silent? If so, it may well have been as you have come through a tough time!

■ PRAYER

Jesus, when we reach out to you in weakness you always respond. You take what we give you, whether good or bad, yet you always give us what is good in return. Clothe us with your joy, so that others may be helped and praise you as well. Amen

Psalm 71:9–15 (NIV)

When we grow old

Do not cast me away when I am old; do not forsake me when my strength is gone. For my enemies speak against me… As for me, I shall always have hope; I will praise you more and more. My mouth will tell of your righteous deeds, of your saving acts all day long— though I know not how to relate them all.

What wonderful words! Are we concerned that we no longer have worth now we are old, or weak, or unable to do much? Perhaps people say horrid or unkind things about us. Maybe we are concerned God will forsake us. The writer of this psalm continued to have hope and planned to praise God even more, in spite of his difficult circumstances. We too can choose whether to listen to those whose words and actions hurt us, or whether to listen to God, who loves us.

The phrase 'all day long' might remind us to praise God often. But it could also remind us of the truth that God's care—his 'saving acts'— really does extend to every hour of each day. Some of us understand only too well, when talking about the past, that experience of not being able 'to relate them all'! We may no longer be able to remember everything, but that does not matter. We can still say that God has done great things for us.

■ **PRAYER**

Thank you for hope, Lord Jesus. When we are worried you might forget us, help us to remember the ways in which you have shown us your love. May we be willing to tell others of all you have done for us. Amen

Colossians 3:15 (NIV)

The peace of Christ

Let the peace of Christ rule in your hearts, since as members of one body you were called to peace. And be thankful.

This Bible verse may be very familiar to you, but I was especially struck by the word 'rule'. We can choose to worry and hang on to our anxieties, or we can let God's peace rule in our hearts. The emphasis here on peace actually *ruling* in our hearts was new to me.

It suggests that God's peace can subdue our unrest, but we certainly have to *allow* God to do that. That means we have to submit to God's ways—and many of us find this difficult. The word 'submission' has a bad press in our world. It's often thought of as a sign of weakness or 'giving in'. Yet Jesus submitted to God, his Father. The Gospels tell us that he always did his Father's will and never pleased himself (John 4:34; 6:38). That's a tall order!

It's not just a matter of being at peace in our personal lives. As we are all part of the same 'body' (or Church), we must be at peace with each other too. Sometimes that also means submitting to others or accepting their point of view. And being thankful is one of God's 'must-haves'; it is more difficult to be thankful if one is not at peace.

■ PRAYER

Lord God, you expect a great deal of us, but in your generosity you provide all the resources we need. Thank you so much. Help us to allow your peace to rule in our lives and to submit joyfully to your word and will in our daily lives. Amen

The Gift of Years

Debbie Thrower is Team Leader of BRF's The Gift of Years ministry and an Anna Chaplain working in care homes. Visit **thegiftofyears.org.uk** to find out more.

Debbie writes...

Welcome to the first issue of *Bible Reflections for Older People*! I'm delighted that you have a copy in your hands and hope you are already deriving enjoyment and, in a quiet way, support from the contents.

In this centre section there are stories, ideas and interviews to pique your interest, encourage you—and help you think about your own attitude to growing older.

I wish you comforting, sometimes surprising, insights as you spend time in company with others, and with the Lord who is 'the same yesterday and today and for ever' (Hebrews 13:8, NIV)—and who never gives up nudging us towards what we *shall* be...

Debbie

Telling the next generation

Thelma Butland, now in her 80s, vividly recalls the weeks of the long summer holidays when she used to look after her grandchildren at her home in Devon. How can we go about sharing our faith with the next generation (while of course keeping them entertained!)?

Acting it out...

To give her grandchildren a focus during their stay, Thelma would choose a Bible story and give everyone a challenge. They were to make the props to go with a simple script, which she would devise for each of them to act out.

'We re-enacted all sorts of stories from the Bible,' Thelma remembers. 'One time, there was the Ark of the Covenant. We made it from cardboard boxes after reading from the book of Exodus (chapter 25). There was also the story of the tumbling walls of Jericho. We made a lot of noise for that one, as you can imagine!'

As well as making all the props and rehearsing the lines for these plays, there was the big climax, of course, when the parents came to collect the junior thespians and the Bible story was played out... in full costume.

Creating good memories

'I've only just turned out the attic and either got rid of, or passed on, various bits and pieces to other people,' said Thelma, as we sat enjoying her memories in her beautiful garden. She has now moved to a bungalow nearer to one of her daughters in Alton, Hampshire. All the offspring remember those summer plays with amusement and affection!

Grandparents have a crucial role

Grandparents have a crucial role to play in passing on the stories of faith, and Thelma's approach has paid dividends. Her family know parts of the Bible of which many other people remain oblivious. It's a lasting gift, a legacy that no one can take away.

Treasures in heaven

Perhaps, in part, that's what Jesus meant in Matthew's Gospel?

'Do not store up for yourselves treasures on earth, where moths and vermin destroy, and where thieves break in and steal. But store up for yourselves treasures in heaven, where moths and vermin do not destroy, and where thieves do not break in and steal.'
Matthew 6:19–20, NIV

Thelma now volunteers to accompany chaplains in their care home visits. She is also an accomplished pianist and enjoys chatting to people after the services.

More recently, though, she had a fall and, at the prospect of needing some respite care herself in one of those very homes, she said (rather ruefully), 'At least I'll know everyone there!'

Characteristically, Thelma is making the best of what is a difficult season in her own life.

Meet Dr Jennifer Bute...

Jennifer Bute is a former missionary and GP. She has lived with dementia for a number of years and her home is a dementia-friendly village in the south-west of England. You may have already enjoyed Jennifer's series of Bible reflections —'Joy for the journey'—in this issue.

Jennifer, why did you become a doctor?

I was fascinated by how the body worked. I had experienced very positive times when in hospital as a young child. Later, I recognised that God had given me the ability to be a doctor—and I never wanted to do anything else.

How did you manage to combine being a doctor with motherhood?

My own mother died when I was four. I always wanted to be there as a mother for my own children, so I took eight years off from my career to invest in their lives until all three were at school—and I don't regret it in any way.

How much experience did you have of dementia before your own diagnosis?

My father had dementia... and I had patients with dementia, but it did not really prepare me. Understanding it from the inside is so different. I had not realised that so much could be done now to improve things.

What was your reaction on being told you had dementia?

Great relief! At last I was believed, and there was a reason for my symptoms: getting horrendously lost, not knowing who people were whom I had known for years, as well as the other memory problems. It had taken five years to get a diagnosis... I used that time to research everything I could so that I could help others. I used to produce health education leaflets, so producing leaflets about dementia was easy for me (all can be downloaded free from my website **www.gloriousopportunity.org**).

How much of a difference has it made to you that you have a faith, and believe that God is involved in these circumstances of your life?

Everything! Nothing is wasted in God's economy. I see my dementia as an unexpected gift from God. Like pain, it's not comfortable, but I believe it is a great privilege for me to understand it from the inside. I am sure dementia has enriched my life. Now living in a dementia-friendly village, I am able to walk this path with so many others and encourage them to find God's love.

How have you turned what most people would regard as a negative into a positive part of your life?

It says in the epistles that if we receive God's gifts with both hands with enthusiasm, it can bring glory to God—but not if we accept the gift through gritted teeth! So I ask God to help me rejoice in adversity, and, in a sense, it has given me a right to speak to others as they see my joy. I believe that we are precious in God's sight and loved by him no matter what the state of our bodies or brains.

What would you say to someone whose relative has dementia and feels like this is 'the beginning of the end'?

I do not assume they will react in the same way as I did. I would reassure them that the relative is, and always will be, 'still there', that feelings remain when facts are forgotten. They always know when they are loved. There is so much that can be done to improve things or help in some way. I would encourage them to help the person continue to socialise, join a memory group, and I would direct them to my website **www.gloriousopportunity.org**; also encourage them to find a support group for themselves, or contact the Admiral Nurses, who support the carers.

What do you think happens to us when we die?

Jesus rose from the dead and I believe we shall also (1 Thessalonians 4:13–18). The Bible says we will sleep and then wake in God's presence and we shall have a new body. I have no fear of death. I believe we shall meet in God's presence in heaven.

How would you sum up your hope for the future?

I have a sure and certain hope. Jesus has gone to prepare a place for us and, as it says in Revelation (21:4), there will be no sorrow, tears or pain in heaven. But meanwhile, until then, I know that Jesus walks with me and I seek to bring a smile to his face in all I do, seeking also to bring hope to those I live among in my dementia-friendly village.

Moving on...

Debbie writes:

I've had a flashback to a time when my late mother had recently moved into residential care. She was finding the change disorientating and was, understandably, lamenting the loss of her old home and garden.

Leaving 'home'

My mother showed me a collection of photos she and one of my sisters had taken for her to keep on the day she left home for good. It had been the family home we'd known for more than 40 years. She had agreed to leave only with the greatest reluctance.

As she leafed through the photos I was suddenly overwhelmed with sadness—and it was I who began to cry. Having tried to be strong for her over the move and all the practicalities, these photo souvenirs proved too much.

Finding comfort

It was the turn of my widowed mother to comfort me and, curiously, in retrospect, it seemed to mark the beginning of her healing from the trauma of leaving the home that she and my father had made together. It was to be a key landmark on that journey of grief for both of us—mother and daughter.

Transforming memories

Memories are part and parcel of our emotional, spiritual, lives. A recollecting, or act of remembrance—'Do this in remembrance of me' (Luke 22:19, NIV)—makes something from the past present once more. This *anamnesis*, as it's called, lies at the heart of the Christian faith.

I think it was when she realised that others were hurting too that my sadly bereft mother was able to see her own pain in clearer perspective. In time, those precious photos became less difficult to view, for her and me.

It may be painful, but sifting through memories can be transformative as well.

Moving day

Like sloughing off a skin
In which I have grown for years,
I leave this house.
Stripped of my personal marks,
It echoes with memories
Of joys and sorrows,
And waits with open heart
To greet its new inhabitants.
And I, temporarily
Possessing nothing, wait
To grow into another home,
To prepare for fresh encounter
With the Holy One.

Ann Lewin (used with permission)

Ann wrote this poem on 1 March 1996. The removal van had left, and she was waiting for a phone call to say she could pick up the keys to her new retirement home.

Decisions, decisions...

Lin Ball

Happily ever after? Is that what you were hoping for after retirement? Perhaps you have longed to be free of the workplace routine for many years. But now that it's arrived or is imminent, it doesn't look as wonderful as you anticipated! Maybe your pension is smaller than you imagined, and your savings have eroded. Or your health is not good. Maybe you're facing these years as a carer, or without a loved one. Or your grandchildren live on the other side of the world. Your picture-perfect dream of your later years is crumbling.

There are decisions to make, with far-reaching implications. Downsize while you've still got some energy—or let the kids sort out the house after you've gone? Fill your days with voluntary work—or settle back and relax? Move into a retirement flat while you can still choose for yourself?

It may be that you feel out of step in an increasingly technological world. Or growing frailty makes you feel vulnerable. Do you worry that your story won't be ending 'happily ever after'?

Making good choices is fundamental to contentment. The Bible assures us that, however difficult our circumstances, we can follow Jesus with a resilience which survives the challenges of everyday life. How can you be a good and godly decision-maker?

Philippians 4:4–7 (NIV)

The cost of worry

Rejoice in the Lord always… The Lord is near. Do not be anxious about anything, but in every situation, by prayer and petition, with thanksgiving, present your requests to God. And the peace of God, which transcends all understanding, will guard your hearts and your minds in Christ Jesus.

An American university professor* asked 1200 older people the question, 'When you look back over your life, what do you most regret?' He expected the answers to be what he calls 'big-ticket items'. Perhaps there had been an affair. Or a business deal that was less than honourable. An addiction. Or perhaps there would be regrets around the tumult of World War II. He was surprised to find that the most common answer was, 'I wish I hadn't spent so much of my life worrying.'

Worry is an enormous waste of time and energy! There are possible outcomes that you can agonise over that may never come to pass. This 'rumination'—as I found it called when I took an online course recently on 'mindfulness'—can cripple our decision-making skills. Constructive problem-solving is different, of course, from worry.

Our trust in God doesn't mean that we shouldn't plan and prepare for our future—but it's why we should do so with a light hand on the tiller. It's a mistake to strive to be the master of our own puny craft.

■ PRAYER

Help me to remember that you, Father God, are the Admiral of the Fleet and are close by. Stormy winds and choppy seas are under your command, and you know the way I should follow. I long to experience more of the peace that comes from trusting you wholly. Amen

* Karl A. Pillemer, Professor of Human Development, Cornell University, USA

Psalm 31:2–5, 14–15 (NIV)

Safely home for the sake of his name

Turn your ear to me… Since you are my rock and my fortress, for the sake of your name lead and guide me… Into your hands I commit my spirit; deliver me, Lord, my faithful God… But I trust in you, Lord; I say, 'You are my God.' My times are in your hands.

How often are we paralysed by fear when faced with a decision that may change the course of our lives or our relationships? In this psalm, the writer appeals to God 'for the sake of your name'. Knowing the character of the God who loves us makes us more able to make choices and decisions with confidence.

The psalmist's conclusion is shared by theologian J.I. Packer. In his bestselling work *Knowing God*, which has sold over a million copies in North America alone, he writes:

> Guidance… is a sovereign act. Not merely does God will to guide us in the sense of showing us his way, that we may tread it; he wills also to guide us in the more fundamental sense of ensuring that, whatever happens, whatever mistakes we may make, we shall come safely home.

Our confidence in his guidance is linked to our understanding of his goodness and his complete integrity. The more we know him, the more we can trust him to guide and protect us, to bring us safely home. When we focus on greater intimacy with God, the way ahead holds no fear; we step out with joy because of our companion.

■ PRAYER
Talk with God about how determined you are to know him better, so that you can be more trusting and certain of his guidance.

Psalm 143:7–10 (NLT)

Landing lights

Come quickly, Lord, and answer me, for my depression deepens. Don't turn away from me, or I will die. Let me hear of your unfailing love each morning, for I am trusting you. Show me where to walk, for I give myself to you… Teach me to do your will, for you are my God. May your gracious Spirit lead me forward on a firm footing.

Having considered God's trustworthiness in guiding us, there are still times when we feel, in all honesty, that we may have missed the way; or when the road is so dark we can't see where to place our feet.

Anne Graham Lotz, daughter of evangelist Billy Graham, uses the illustration of the lights that must be kept in a straight line when an aeroplane is landing at night. To know we are in the centre of God's will, she says, the four lights that must be lined up are God's word, inner conviction, personal circumstances and the counsel of mature godly friends. That's a great checklist!

- Does the Bible have anything to say about this decision?
- What does my heart—inhabited by the Holy Spirit—tell me?
- What makes sense of where I am right now and what I've been through to be here?
- What advice can Christian friends give me?

If there is recognisable agreement across the answers, we can have certainty as we step out!

■ PRAYER

When I'm feeling low and in the dark, help me not to be dismayed, O loving God, but to line up the landing lights you have given to guide me in the right way. Amen

John 10:3–5 (NLT)

A familiar voice

'The gatekeeper opens the gate for him, and the sheep recognise his voice and come to him. He calls his own sheep by name and leads them out. After he has gathered his own flock, he walks ahead of them, and they follow him because they know his voice. They won't follow a stranger; they will run from him because they don't know his voice.'

Having worked for a sight loss charity, I have a number of friends who are blind, three of whom go to my church. When I approach one of them for a chat after the service I usually say, 'Good morning, it's Lin.' It feels polite to give my name to someone with sight loss. But I know it's not really needed. They identify my voice immediately because they know me quite well.

How I wish it was like that with me and God! I long for the day when I know him well enough that when he speaks I identify him immediately. Of course, it's unlikely I'll hear a real voice. But I do believe that God speaks, and we need to listen and become familiar with his voice.

The picture of the sheep and the shepherd in John chapter 10 is reassuring, although the setting is alien to most of us. If only there was an equivalent story told by Jesus of people hearing his voice in a crowded supermarket or an echoing railway station! Our lives are often deafeningly cluttered with noise, so we find it hard to distinguish the voice of the Master.

■ PRAYER
Talk to God about the many voices competing for your attention when you want to hear him clearly. Ask for his help in paying attention to his voice above all others.

Matthew 26:36–39 (NIV)

The surrendered heart

Then Jesus went with his disciples to a place called Gethsemane…
and he began to be sorrowful and troubled. Then he said to them,
'My soul is overwhelmed with sorrow to the point of death.'… Going
a little farther, he fell with his face to the ground and prayed, 'My
Father, if it is possible, may this cup be taken from me. Yet not as
I will, but as you will.'

Here is Jesus at the moment of his greatest challenge as he prayed in Gethsemane in anticipation of betrayal and a shameful and barbaric death. Surely if Jesus needed to submit to his Father over the way ahead, how much more must we know something of that submission! Seeking guidance is to do with submission of the heart, a laying aside of our wishes in preference to his.

Waiting is frequently a companion to submission. We often feel that God is keeping us waiting and we can't see why. His timescales bear little relation to ours. Often, too, it seems that he is economical with his guidance. A little candlelight is shed on our way just one step at a time when we would rather a powerful spotlight illuminated the road for miles ahead—and we struggle with being kept in the dark.

Waiting, submitting, accepting—all are part of the experience of following Christ. But don't imagine that these attitudes are passive. Far from it! Sometimes it takes real courage and determination to wait on God.

■ PRAYER

Are you facing a difficult decision or waiting to know the way ahead?
Meditate with purpose on these words from Psalm 37: 'Be still before
the Lord and wait patiently for him' (v. 7, NIV).

Romans 12:1–2 (MSG)

On an adventure

Take your everyday, ordinary life—your sleeping, eating, going-to-work, and walking-around life—and place it before God as an offering. Embracing what God does for you is the best thing you can do for him… fix your attention on God. You'll be changed from the inside out. Readily recognise what he wants from you, and quickly respond to it.

An attitude of following God starts in the mind. It's a decision in itself. Don't assume that decision-making with God is unadventurous. As Mr Beaver tells the children in C.S. Lewis' *The Lion, the Witch and the Wardrobe*, the Lion isn't safe—'But he's good. He's the King.' And God doesn't father a community of clones. Be prepared that sometimes the way will feel insecure, risky. And know that the path he leads us on will probably be different from that being followed by others we know—and that's all right!

The church I attend is asking the question, 'Should we take out the pews to create a more flexible worship space?' Yes, we know that lots of other churches have been this way. But we have to make our own decision, rather than adopt some other church's choice. As a friend said to me, 'The only person who welcomes change is a wet baby!' Whatever the outcome—whether we invest in stackable chairs or preserve the polished pews—the decision's going to take courage.

■ PRAYER

Father, life is full of decisions, and I know that older people tend to be more and more risk-averse. Even putting off a decision is a decision! Help me face with confidence the decisions around change in my life—and help me to embrace the adventure of it all. Amen

John 16:13–14 (NIV)

The holy satnav

But when he, the Spirit of truth, comes, he will guide you into all the truth. He will not speak on his own; he will speak only what he hears, and he will tell you what is yet to come. He will glorify me because it is from me that he will receive what he will make known to you.

Some people have a healthy scepticism about satnavs. I confess to having an unhealthy trust in mine! I call her Grace ('Grace will lead me home' says the hymn!*). Once or twice, I admit, Grace has led me down some muddy cart track in the middle of nowhere. But she's also got me out of countless scrapes over road closures and unpredictable diversions. As a journalist, I've had to drive many 'one-off' trips to interview someone I'd never have to meet again. It seemed an unnecessary burden on the brain cells to wrestle with the map for a journey I'd never repeat; hence my total reliance on my satnav.

'I will not leave you comfortless' is a phrase I always remember from the King James Version (John 14:18). There are many twists in the road of life. But we are not alone. The Holy Spirit, who comes to live within us when we give our lives to Jesus, is our comforter and guide. It's his role to interpret the Father's will to us, like some holy satnav—but this one truly is completely infallible! Knowing the Spirit is within gives us the confidence we need to step out into the unknown.

■ **PRAYER**

Thank you, Father God, for the guiding, comforting Holy Spirit—your gift to me for the times when the way ahead isn't clear. Amen

---

* John Newton, 'Amazing Grace', 1779

Psalm 119:103–105 (CEV)

Following the map

Your teachings are sweeter than honey. They give me understanding and make me hate all lies. Your word is a lamp that gives light wherever I walk.

When I formally retired (writers never do really retire!), I became a member of the Leicestershire Footpaths Association. For a few pounds a year I can choose from a programme of over 150 guided walks every year of between six and ten miles. Being geographically challenged, I have found myself walking up hill and down dale, all over the county, and often not at all sure where I was. But I put my faith in the group leader who a) is an experienced walker, b) has pre-walked the route and c) is carrying the map. Sometimes you may wonder if you are lost—but actually you are quite safe, and discovering a new and beautiful path.

Wanting to take God's path rather than make our own choices becomes second nature the more we love to read the Bible. It's not that the Bible reveals our future—though sometimes it does. But the Bible shows us the all-powerful, all-knowing God who is totally *for* us, completely committed to us, bound to us by steadfast love. The Bible reassures us that he will never leave us or forsake us, that he works all things for our good. The Bible is not a crystal ball, but a revelation of God's love for us here and now that enables us to face whatever is ahead.

■ PRAYER
Father God, teach me to know and love your word—and may my experience be that your word gives the light I need for the way ahead. Amen

Exodus 13:21–22 (NLT)

The blessed ordinary

The Lord went ahead of them. He guided them during the day with a pillar of cloud, and he provided light at night with a pillar of fire. This allowed them to travel by day or by night. And the Lord did not remove the pillar of cloud or pillar of fire from its place in front of the people.

When I read this story, I am struck by how God guides appropriately. For those people, at that time, the pillars of fire and cloud were the appropriate guidance. For the astrologers searching out the infant Jesus, the appropriate guidance was a bright star.

Sometimes we think guidance needs to be supernatural—and on occasion it is. But more often, especially as we mature, guidance is in the ordinary. The star wouldn't be ordinary for us, but it was for the astrologers.

So, within the remits of knowing the character of God and researching the wisdom of the Bible, we sometimes find guidance by exercising the plain and simple common sense with which God has gifted us. In the absence of a burning bush or writing on the wall, we are expected to weigh up the pros and cons and just choose. 'Life is a sum of all your choices,' said French philosopher Albert Camus. And indeed it is. To distress ourselves with the 'what ifs' of what cannot be undone is to waste precious energy and divert us from the 'what is' of today.

■ PRAYER

'If any of you lacks wisdom, you should ask God, who gives generously to all without finding fault, and it will be given to you' (James 1:5, NIV). Pray for wisdom that's equal to the decisions you need to make.

Isaiah 30:19–21 (CEV)

There is only today

The Lord is kind, and as soon as he hears your cries for help, he will come. The Lord has given you trouble and sorrow as your food and drink. But now... he will guide you. Whether you turn to the right or to the left, you will hear a voice saying, 'This is the road! Now follow it.'

These scripture verses remind me that following Jesus is not a bed of roses. Or if it is, the roses have thorns! Yet the thorns are not mistakes, but part of the path. Troubles are not a sign of having missed the way. There may be difficulties for a season. But the end of the journey, for the believer, is always perfect and glorious.

If you are worried about the future, if its uncertainties are distressing you, fix your eyes on Jesus and fix them on today. Resolve to follow Jesus today, to live honestly and in a way that honours him. Your destination is sure, even though the way is unknown.

'Yesterday is gone. Tomorrow has not yet come. We have only today. Let us begin.' That was said by Mother Teresa (1910–97), the Albanian Catholic nun who gave her life to helping the desperately poor in Calcutta, India. Take courage. Be decisive. God is with you.

■ PRAYER
What decisions, large or small, are you facing today? Lay them before God. Express your praise of God as the Father who cares about you deeply and for ever. Thank him that you can trust him implicitly with whatever lies ahead.

Rhythms of remembrance

Russ Parker

Recently, I revisited my childhood home for the first time in 41 years. I went into the bedroom where I once shared a bed with two of my brothers. I met my old neighbour Mrs Dodd, now 90 years old. She told me stories of things I had almost forgotten. We laughed and we cried as we remembered what we had all been through, and the years melted away as we rediscovered each other. I came away knowing that I had learnt more about myself, and I valued more deeply the gifts that I had been given.

The Bible has over 160 references to remembering and they fall into two general categories: God remembering us and our needs for flourishing; and our remembering of what God has done for us. Both acts of remembrance invite us to reconnect with renewed appreciation to the presence and grace of God in our lives. These reflections are an exploration of how our 'God memories' are a living resource for faith-building in times of difficulty and challenge, when it is all too easy to forget the Lord who shares our journey.

Joshua 4:6–7 (CEV)

Stones of remembrance

Someday your children will ask, 'Why are these rocks here?' Then you can tell them how the water stopped flowing when the chest was being carried across the river. These rocks will always remind our people of what happened here today.

In the cemetery of an ancient parish church on the Dingle peninsular stands a large, granite tombstone dedicated to John Moriarty, a much-loved minister. Carved in the stone is a coracle, signifying that he has gone on his final journey after 40 years of dedicated service. It stands as a testament to his legacy of service, from which the congregation still derives encouragement.

Similarly, as the Israelites crossed the River Jordan, Joshua took twelve stones from the middle of the river and placed them on the banks of their new land. These reminded Israel of the faithfulness of God who had delivered them from slavery and brought them to the Promised Land (v. 9). The stones were also an inspiration and encouragement to build their lives on this truth: that the God who had dried up the River Jordan was still with them powerfully.

We all need reminding of those times when God stepped into our lives to help, heal and guide us. The challenges of life sometimes undermine our faith and we need to stay connected to what God has done for us and draw fresh fire from this. Perhaps you could build your own version of stones of remembrance. Why not write down a list of times when God met you at your point of need? Spend a few moments remembering them quietly.

■ PRAYER
Help me, Lord, to remember those times when you were there for me so I can live in the strength of your presence now. Amen

Exodus 20:8, 11 (NIV)

Remember to rest

Remember the Sabbath day by keeping it holy… For in six days the Lord made the heavens and the earth, the sea, and all that is in them, but he rested on the seventh day. Therefore the Lord blessed the Sabbath day and made it holy.

You may be familiar with the response of the child who, upon hearing this Bible text read out in church, asked, 'Was God tired after creating the heavens and the earth, and that was why he needed a rest day?'

It is important to know that the word 'rest' in the Bible is not about recovering from weariness, but about finishing well. When God completed his work of creation he needed to add no more to it—and so he finished well. When Jesus invites us to come to him for rest when we are weary and burdened, it is an invitation to finish looking elsewhere for our salvation and healing (Matthew 11:28–29). The sabbath day, therefore, is an opportunity to finish well from the labours of the week—and rest.

Exodus 20:10 tells us that this holy rest is for the hired servants and slaves, as well as the masters. The sabbath is also about honouring the rights of others. This special day is a chance not just to leave work and renew lost energy, but to begin the new week well with celebration of God, time for family and appreciation of the world in which we live. 'God woos us to rest so we can find our worth in who we are and not what we do' (Barbara Brown Taylor).

■ PRAYER
O God my Father, teach me to find my rest in you and not in what I do. Amen

Luke 23:39–43 (MSG)

Remember who I am

One of the criminals… cursed him: 'Some Messiah you are! Save yourself! Save us!' But the other one made him shut up: 'Have you no fear of God?… We deserve this, but not him—he did nothing to deserve this.' Then he said, 'Jesus, remember me when you enter your kingdom.' He said, 'Don't worry, I will. Today you will join me in paradise.'

This is an amazing story of confession and hope. The second thief knew that Jesus was innocent and that he was guilty. Unlike his co-thief, he didn't demand a last-minute rescue from punishment; he just asked to be remembered. He also had the conviction that there was more to Jesus than just a crucified preacher. He knew that Jesus' death was the beginning of something more, not the end of another failed dreamer. Consequently, he asks to be remembered when Jesus enters his kingdom.

Whatever ugliness, shame and disappointments summed up this man's life, he wanted to be assured that someone thought his life mattered. How stunned he must have been when Jesus responded by saying, 'Don't worry, I will. Today you will join me in paradise'! He doesn't bargain or try to vindicate his life of crime; he simply asks Jesus to see him as a person, to look deeper than his deeds and to see his humanity. When he said 'Remember me,' he was asking Jesus to mark the fact that he had lived, that he mattered.

We all need to know this. Be encouraged, therefore, that no matter whether or not our lives are successful, Jesus remembers who we really are—a special person for whom he gave his life on the cross.

■ **PRAYER**

Thank you, Lord, for remembering who I am. Amen

Nehemiah 13:22 (NIV)

Remember what I have done

Remember me for this also, my God, and show mercy to me according to your great love.

At a healing service for a church that had been through hard times, I thanked one of the ministers for his faithful service. The congregation gave him a standing ovation. He was reduced to tears of gratitude and told me how blessed he felt to be so appreciated.

Nehemiah was an outstanding risk-taker for God. He was tasked with rebuilding the ruined city of Jerusalem, which had lain destroyed and derelict for 70 years. He galvanised a demoralised community into taking part and they worked around the clock to erect the city walls. He faced the opposition of local warlords, who tried to intimidate him and sent false reports about him to the king so that Nehemiah was ordered to stop building. He had to revive the faith of the priests, who had given up on God. Through it all he persevered, and eventually Jerusalem was rebuilt and worship was relaunched in the temple.

The secret of Nehemiah's achievement, however, was what lay behind the scenes. He constantly looked to God to remember him with favour and to appreciate the work he had done. In fact, at least five times he asks God to remember him—and encourages the people to remember God (1:8, 4:14; 5:19; 13:14; 13:22; 13:31). Whether from insecurity or reliance upon God, Nehemiah found strength in being remembered and appreciated by God for what he was doing for him. We too can be encouraged! For God sees our work—even when others do not—and he is the first to cheer for us.

■ **PRAYER**

Thank you, Lord, for celebrating what I do for you. Amen

Isaiah 43:25 (NIV)

Remembers your sins no more...

I, even I, am he who blots out your transgressions, for my own sake, and remembers your sins no more.

Sometimes our problem is that we are not always able to put the memory of our misdemeanours aside. When we fail or fall again, we are tempted to doubt whether God has really forgiven us for all that has gone before!

The astonishing truth about this Bible verse is that it describes God's intention to forgive the sins of Israel—even when that nation continued to turn its back on God. God doesn't wait for Israel to repent before making his incredible offer. Three times Isaiah refers to the fact that the nation had not sought God for his forgiveness (43:22–24). So this verse shows the determination of God to be the one who forgives sins and to do it utterly, completely and without reservation.

He forgives for his 'own sake', because this is his heart's default position, not because we deserve it. Isaiah states that God *chooses* not to remember our sins. This is because, while it is impossible for God to forget, choosing not to remember is an act of generous grace. I love the quote from the Dutch author Corrie ten Boom, who was commenting upon Micah 7:19, where we are told that our pardoning God has thrown our sins into the depths of the sea. She goes on to write that then God set up a sign that said, 'No fishing allowed'!

■ **PRAYER**

Thank you, Lord, that you have chosen not to remember my sins and call me to live free of them. Amen

Matthew 5:23–24 (NIV)

Remembering as worship

Therefore, if you are offering your gift at the altar and there remember that your brother or sister has something against you, leave your gift there in front of the altar. First go and be reconciled to them; then come and offer your gift.

Most of us carry regrets about how we have hurt others, who may still carry those wounds. The context of this passage is the Sermon on the Mount, where Jesus is warning of the toxic effects that come from the breakdown of relationships that then go on to fester.

Jesus points out that it is when we come seeking God in worship that we remember the healing needs of those we have hurt. It is also in worship that we fully know that God has forgiven *us*. The challenge then is to go and work for reconciliation with the other person, not from the motivation of proving we are not that bad really, but as a continuation of our worship of God.

I have much admired the work of Rhiannon Lloyd, who has been used to facilitate healing and reconciliation between the Hutu and Tutsi peoples in Rwanda. She begins her work by telling everyone that, being Welsh, she hated the English for their dominance of her people and culture. However, if God had forgiven her sins, what right did she have to hold the sins of the English against them? Such an insight transformed her life. Whether by letter or by personal contact, may the Lord help you to start a journey of healing and reconciliation with the people who need to hear from you.

■ **PRAYER**

Dear Father, help me to remember those with whom I need to be reconciled and help me to know what to do next. Amen

2 Timothy 2:8–9 (NIV)

Remember Jesus Christ

Remember Jesus Christ, raised from the dead, descended from David. This is my gospel, for which I am suffering even to the point of being chained like a criminal. But God's word is not chained.

Every now and then we need a wake-up call about Jesus Christ. We need to beware of settling for a Christ who is like a superhero, for whom the cross was a piece of cake. The Jesus whom the apostle Paul calls us to remember is the one who screamed out his pain of abandonment on the cross—but who then rose from the dead, bringing us life. In stating that Jesus was descended from David, Paul emphasises that while he is both fully human and historical, he is also the Messiah. Paul paid a high price for not settling for a lesser version of Jesus to suit the spirit of the age.

Remembering Jesus also brings us in touch with what he has done for us. Because he suffered death on the cross and has risen, he understands our sufferings and can tell us we are not alone in these. Such thoughts inspired hymn-writer William Young Fullerton's words:

I cannot tell how silently he suffered,
As with his peace he graced this place of tears,
Or how his heart upon the cross was broken,
The crown of pain to three and thirty years.
But this I know, he heals the broken-hearted,
And stays our sin, and calms our lurking fear,
And lifts the burden from the heavy laden,
For yet the Saviour, Saviour of the world, is here.

■ PRAYER

Dear Lord Jesus, help us to remember that you are not above us, but with us. Amen

Psalm 77:6, 9, 11–12 (NIV)

Remember your songs in the night

I remembered my songs in the night. My heart meditated and my spirit asked… 'Has God forgotten to be merciful?'… I will remember the deeds of the Lord; yes, I will remember your miracles of long ago. I will consider all your works and meditate on all your mighty deeds.

How many times have you been told to 'sleep on it'? It refers to those times when you are trying to sort something out and are getting nowhere. However, after a night's sleep we often wake up with a solution!

There is an ancient belief that when we sleep our souls are wide awake in our dreams. The fact that the Bible contains over 200 references to dreams and visions might seem to bear this out! However, the night is also regarded as the time when we are most alone in spiritual battle, as we have no companions to support us. This is, perhaps, why the Bible uses graphic descriptions of the night as spiritual darkness and refers to the 'terror of night' and the 'pestilence that stalks in the darkness' (Psalm 91:5–6, NIV). Perhaps the reason why Paul and Silas chose to sing at midnight in the Philippian jail was to dispel and break the power of their spiritual attacker (Acts 16:25).

The psalmist knew what it was to be harassed as he tried to sleep. In order to overcome his depressing thoughts, he learnt to remember all the ways God had been with him in the past. If you have trouble sleeping, ask God to give you songs in the night, reminders of those times he has helped and encouraged you.

■ **PRAYER**

Thank you, Lord, that you give me songs in the night to remind me that you are always with me. Amen

Philippians 1:3–6 (NIV)

Remember to thank

I thank my God every time I remember you… being confident of this, that he who began a good work in you will carry it on to completion until the day of Christ Jesus.

Do you remember to thank God for others? Eight times Paul begins his letters to the churches by thanking God for them. This was true even of the Corinthian church, which was in a near-chaotic state. Celebration mustn't be confused with flattery!

Paul is celebrating the churches, first because they belong to Christ and, second, because of their acts of faithfulness. Jesus was celebrated by his Father at his baptism before he had preached any sermons, made any disciples or performed any miracles (Mark 1:11). He was celebrated for who he was more than what he had done. Then there is the example of Barnabas, who saw potential in the young man John Mark (Acts 15:37–39). Paul would not work with him because he had failed in his ministry, but Barnabas sticks with him. And years later, when Paul is in prison and needs support and encouragement, it's John Mark he sends for because this young man had now matured to become a seasoned disciple (2 Timothy 4:11).

Remember, what we do *not* celebrate shrinks through lack of affirmation! Let us be people who celebrate and encourage each other. Ask God to give you insight into the potential in others and give thanks for them and celebrate them. To be encouraged in this way helps us all to take heart in times of darkness and challenge, and enables us to step into more of what God has for us.

■ PRAYER

Help me, O Lord, to remember those who need to receive my thanks and teach me to celebrate them. Amen

Psalm 105:42–44 (MSG)

God remembers his promises

He remembered… his promise to Abraham, his servant. Remember this! He led his people out singing for joy; his chosen people marched, singing their hearts out! He made them a gift of the country they entered.

Madame Thérèse Pailla was stunned to receive a letter that had been posted to her home in France 138 years earlier, addressed to her great-grandmother. The French postal service apologised for the delay in its arrival! My friend Bruce Brodowski, whose father died in 1945, just before Bruce was born, travelled to Margraten in the Netherlands to visit the site of his father's grave for the first time. His father had been a tank commander who was killed while trying to help a family to escape danger. He had not been forgotten and there were commemorative plaques to his name in the town. It greatly helped to heal Bruce's heartache concerning the father he had never known.

We can imagine the joy and surprise of the captive Hebrews, then, when, after a silence of nearly 450 years, God showed up to tell them that they were not forgotten. They were not only remembered, but they were delivered from captivity as God led them out of Egypt, keeping his promise to their ancient ancestor, Abraham. The psalmist encourages us to hold on to our memories of God's faithfulness so that we remain true to our faith and destiny. Whether God is silent or noticeably active in our lives, he never forgets what is important for our good. Let's remember that and rejoice!

■ PRAYER

Dear Father, thank you that you never forget the promises you have made to us. Help us to cherish those memories so that they may feed our faith today. Amen

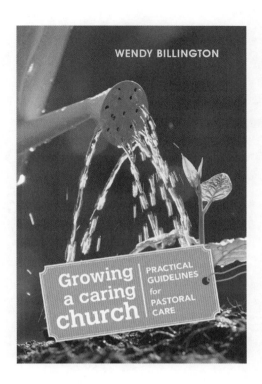

Earthed in Jesus' command that as his disciples we are to love one another, this book speaks to all of us—from church pastors to those attending—but specifically to home group leaders and members. It shows how home groups can be places where people's pain and difficulties are noticed, and first steps taken to help. Wendy Billington offers valuable insights coupled with realistic and practical advice, drawing on her years of pastoral work in the community and in the local church.

Growing a Caring Church
Practical guidelines for pastoral care
Wendy Billington
978 0 85746 799 0 £6.99
brfonline.org.uk

Bible readings for special times

Ill Health
Wendy Bray

Whether we are going through a period of being house-bound through ill health or facing a short or longer stay in hospital, we can find help and consolation in the Bible. This book offers 24 undated reflections drawing on a range of relevant Bible passages, and offering ways of connecting more closely with God and drawing strength, peace and security from the knowledge of his presence with us.

Ill Health
Wendy Bray
978 0 85746 231 2 £3.99
brfonline.org.uk

Bereavement

Jean Watson

This book of 24 undated reflections draws comfort and inspiration from the Bible and from experience for those who are going through a time of bereavement, as well as providing insight for those wanting to support others who are bereaved. Jean Watson suggests how it might feel to get through the dark days and to move, however slowly, from 'getting by' with help, to 'getting a life' in which living with loss goes alongside the gains in terms of new insights on faith and life and a greater ability to empathise with others.

Bereavement
Jean Watson
978 0 85746 326 5 £3.99
brfonline.org.uk

To order

Online: **brfonline.org.uk**
Telephone: +44 (0)1865 319700
Mon–Fri 9.15–17.30
Post: complete this form and send to the address below

Delivery times within the UK are normally 15 working days. Prices are correct at the time of going to press but may change without prior notice.

Title	Issue*	Price	Qty	Total
Growing a Caring Church		£6.99		
Ill Health		£3.99		
Bereavement		£3.99		
Bible Reflections for Older People (single copy)	Jan/May* 17	£4.99		
Bible Reflections for Older People (10–24 copies)	Jan/May* 17	£4.75		
Bible Reflections for Older People (25–49 copies)	Jan/May* 17	£4.50		
Bible Reflections for Older People (50 or more copies)	Jan/May* 17	£3.99		

delete as appropriate

POSTAGE AND PACKING CHARGES			
Order value	UK	Europe	Rest of world
Under £7.00	£1.25	£3.00	£5.50
£7.00–£29.99	£2.25	£5.50	£10.00
£30.00 and over	FREE	Prices on request	

Total value of books	
Postage and packing	
Total for this order	

Please complete in BLOCK CAPITALS

Title .... First name/initials .... Surname..

Address ....

.... Postcode ....

Acc. No. .... Telephone ....

Email ....

Method of payment

☐ Cheque (made payable to BRF) ☐ MasterCard / Visa

Card no. ☐☐☐☐ ☐☐☐☐ ☐☐☐☐ ☐☐☐☐

Valid from ☐☐ ☐☐ Expires ☐☐ ☐☐ Security code* ☐☐☐

Last 3 digits on the reverse of the card

Signature* .... Date .... / .... / ....

*ESSENTIAL IN ORDER TO PROCESS YOUR ORDER

Please return this form to:

BRF, 15 The Chambers, Vineyard, Abingdon OX14 3FE | enquiries@brf.org.uk

To read our terms and conditions, please visit **brfonline.org.uk/terms**.

The Bible Reading Fellowship (BRF) is a Registered Charity (233280)

BIBLE REFLECTIONS FOR OLDER PEOPLE GROUP SUBSCRIPTION FORM

All our Bible reading notes can be ordered online
by visiting **biblereadingnotes.org.uk/subscriptions**

The group subscription rate for *Bible Reflections for Older People* will be £14.97 per person until April 2018.

☐ I would like to take out a group subscription for .... (*quantity*) copies.

☐ Please start my order with the May 2017 / September 2017 / January 2018* issue. I would like to pay annually/receive an invoice with each edition of the notes.* (*delete as appropriate*)

Please do not send any money with your order. Send your order to BRF and we will send you an invoice. The group subscription year is from 1 May to 30 April. If you start subscribing in the middle of a subscription year we will invoice you for the remaining number of issues left in that year.

Name and address of the person organising the group subscription:

Title .... First name/initials .... Surname...

Address ....

.... Postcode ....

Telephone .... Email ....

Church ....

Name of minister ....

Name and address of the person paying the invoice if the invoice needs to be sent directly to them:

Title .... First name/initials .... Surname...

Address ....

.... Postcode ....

Telephone .... Email ....

Please return this form to:
BRF, 15 The Chambers, Vineyard, Abingdon OX14 3FE | enquiries@brf.org.uk
To read our terms and conditions, please visit **brfonline.org.uk/terms**.

BROP0117   The Bible Reading Fellowship is a Registered Charity (233280)

BIBLE REFLECTIONS FOR OLDER PEOPLE INDIVIDUAL/GIFT SUBSCRIPTION FORM

To order online, please visit **biblereadingnotes.org.uk/subscriptions**

☐ I would like to take out a subscription (*complete your name and address details only once*)
☐ I would like to give a gift subscription (*please provide both names and addresses*)

Title .... First name/initials .... Surname..

Address ....

.... Postcode ....

Telephone .... Email ....

Gift subscription name ....

Gift subscription address ....

.... Postcode ....

Gift message (*20 words max. or include your own gift card*):

....

....

Please send **Bible Reflections for Older People** beginning with the May 2017 / September 2017 / January 2018 issue (*delete as appropriate*):

(*please tick box*)	UK	Europe	Rest of world
Bible Reflections for Older People	☐ £18.75	☐ £26.70	☐ £30.75

Total enclosed £ .... (*cheques should be made payable to 'BRF'*)

Please charge my MasterCard / Visa ☐ Debit card ☐ with £ ....

Card no. ☐☐☐☐ ☐☐☐☐ ☐☐☐☐ ☐☐☐☐

Valid from [M][M] [Y][Y] Expires [M][M] [Y][Y] Security code* ☐☐☐
Last 3 digits on the reverse of the card

Signature* .... Date ..../......./.......

*ESSENTIAL IN ORDER TO PROCESS YOUR ORDER

Please return this form to:
BRF, 15 The Chambers, Vineyard, Abingdon OX14 3FE | enquiries@brf.org.uk
To read our terms and conditions, please visit brfonline.org.uk/terms.

The Bible Reading Fellowship is a Registered Charity (233280)